THE PROCESS

A Guide to Finding Your Path and Creating Lasting Positive Change

CHARLIE MINANNO, MBA, CPA, CISA CPBA

Publishing Assistance Provided by:

Michelle Morrow www.chellreads.com

Contents

To all who are reading this book, your journey has started. We have all come here for different reasons. We are all looking for change. Some of us are looking for monumental life-altering changes and some of us are looking to make some small improvements. Some of us are desperate for change and don't know where to look next. Whatever brought you here, the change you desire awaits you. May you attain your highest potential and may you and all of your loved ones experience the happiness that is found inside of you.

Acknowledgments

Writing this book has been a journey for me. It has been a process. A process of ups and downs- a process of change. A process that started long before this book was ever imagined. I am indebted to many people who indirectly and directly brought me to this point.

I am most grateful to **my mother, Charlotte**, for always believing in me and teaching me that there is no normal and it was ok to expand my thinking beyond just "normal" perceptions of reality. I have been and still am the benefactor of your suffering. I miss you Mom.

Bowser – Gratitude does not do enough justice to how eternally thankful I am to have been a part of your life for twelve plus years. Our relationship goes way beyond our time together and there are so many other things I would like to tell you but you already know this. Thank you for manifesting yourself to me. I can't wait to see you again!

Woody – You too taught me many lessons. I am blessed to have shared a mutual road on our individual paths that quickly became entangled. I am sorry for your suffering and thank you for your resilience.

To my brother **Joe** – Thank you for always looking out for me and being someone I can always turn to when I need something. Thank you for putting up with my shit and always being a great big brother. For as long as I live, I will fondly remember our times of watching TV and movies together, like Psych, Fringe, People of Earth and Twin Peaks. You have provided me a safe place to relax, be comfortable and work towards my goals. Thank you!

Grammi – Thank you for always taking care of me and putting us first. You are one in a million. I can't wait to see you again!

Beata - Thank you for constantly supporting me. You always pushed me to finish this book and stick with it. I guess tough love works (sometimes, not all the times)! You have taught me many lessons and your resilience continues to amaze me. Your incandescence is pure radiance illuminated.

Pops – Thank for being there for me and always being yourself. Your uniqueness rivals that of no one. I look forward to watching Lonesome Dove with you for many years to come.

Maia – Thanks for letting me into your life. I still remember bunkin bonuts and everything in between now and then. I am so proud of the woman that you have become!

Sang – My first mentor - Thank you for being there for me for so long. May our brainstorming sessions continue for years.

Tom – Thank you for letting me into your family and helping me through navigate muddy waters. Thanks for being my best friend.

Kristen – Our path to friendship has been non-traditional. It amazes me how our connection has developed so organically. Our continued support for each other is something I look forward to for many years to come.

Doyle – Thanks for being there for me all these years! I am proud to call you my oldest friend.

Alan – Thank you for listening to me complain all these years and helping me navigate through the difficult times.

Karna – I miss you bro. Thanks for coming into my life, when I needed you most. See you soon brother.

Jeff – Thanks for being a constant sounding board. I look forward to the continued evolution of our friendship.

Aunt Helen and Uncle John – My fondest childhood memories are summers spent with you, Uncle Ziggy, and Aunt Marie in Connecticut. Thank you for being so good to me and our family, especially my mom. I will always remember you visiting my mom and checking in with her, during her most challenging times – Thank you!

Bill P – Thank you for your constant and consistent support and true friendship, dating all the way back to kindergarten.

Thanks to all my friends who have supported for many years. I hope this mutual support will continue for years to come. Thank you to Fabio, Christine, Jason, Miller, Anna, Rob F and Al M.

Artists, organizations, and others who have inspired me: Jenifer Shapiro, Justin Warfield, Richard Rudd, Eben Pagan, David Lynch, Malcolm Gladwell, Tom Best, Nourishing Storm Care – Hatboro, PA, Extreme Karate-Rockledge, PA, Americks-Willow Grove, PA, and Twin Oaks, IC - Louisa, Virginia

DISCOVER YOUR PATH, DEFINE YOUR IDEAL LIFE AND LIVE IT FULLY!

All of us have some type of change we are hoping to achieve. Sometimes we are consciously aware of what we want and sometimes it is lurking in the background. In order to live the life you want, you have to consciously design your life first.

In *THE PROCESS*, you will find very methodical and practical techniques that will help you define and achieve the lasting change you desire- change that is aligned with your unique gifts and talents and more importantly aligned with your core values and beliefs.

THE PROCESS provides you with motivation, background, mindset, theory and practical step by step instructions that you can use to help in making any change you desire. *THE PROCESS* is a stand-alone workbook style book that can be used individually or in a group setting. It is also a great complement to other books associated with Neuro Linguistic Programming (NLP).

Chapter 1

PERSONAL INTRODUCTION

"You have to imagine how you want things to be, then you can change them." – "You got to try something…. right?"

Quote from a young Peter Bishop - fictional character on the television show *Fringe*

Mid-April 2013 - A Thursday afternoon

"What the fuck? I don't think this is good. In fact, I know it's not good – something is fucked up. Why would the doctor say it might be cancer but tell me he wasn't sure?" is what I said in a very confused and at the same time frightened voice to Jeff, one of my best friends and colleagues since college. In his cool and calm manner, he told me not to get ahead of myself and not to jump to conclusions.   He volunteered to take the afternoon off to meet me at Starbucks and brainstorm with me about what was going on.   I wasn't about to refuse his offer. Two hours later, while at Starbucks with Jeff, I received a call from the doctor. My appointment that was supposed to be in five weeks was moved to tomorrow, Friday, at 5 PM.   The receptionist did not ask me if that time worked for me; she just told me to be there. Oh, she also said to stop by the office within the next hour to pick up a script for bloodwork and a chest x-ray.   It was official – I was definitely fucked in some manner and not a manner of the enjoyable variety.

Fast forward five days later and now my testicle count is at one versus the two it was just a week earlier – testicular cancer at 36. Because of that event, my life has changed in very meaningful ways. I had to make some very tough treatment decisions, with the support of my family, namely my brother Joe, and my friends as well. I had to challenge the authoritative directives of multiple doctors who insisted I needed "preventative" chemotherapy and follow my own treatment path that went against conventional medicine's guidelines.

Sometime in the late 2010s

As I write this, it is many years later, and I am still cancer free, without chemotherapy or any other type of Western medical intervention, other than the initial surgery to remove the tumor.

One of the most interesting results from this experience was how many personal changes, challenges, and new endeavors took place during the timeframe following my initial diagnosis with cancer. What was even more amazing was how effortless these changes and the related motivation to make such changes appeared to be. During this time-frame, just after my cancer diagnosis, motivation for any type of positive change was virtually limitless and available on-call to me for at least six months from my diagnosis.

I noticed, however, that after around this six-month period (and a few clean cancer-free CT scans later), my focus and motivation started to decline. The decline certainly was not drastic, and there were certain beneficial personal changes that were evident as being permanent lifestyle changes, but not all of the initial changes had such a sense of permanency.

As a result of this, I have had a constant lingering question in the back of my head: How can motivation be synthesized or created in the absence of a life-changing event? After going through my health challenges, I gained first-hand insight into the power of effortless motivation. I also witnessed life happen, as they say, and saw this motivation wane, to a certain extent. When this depletion of motivation first started to occur, I felt that I could re-enlist and call upon such motivation and the related positive changes at any point, but the truth was that despite my formal training in psychology and Neuro Linguistic Programming (NLP), I was still unable to magically re-enlist such positive motivation strategies on demand. I often fell into unresourceful and destructive behaviors and struggled to make good decisions. Everyone thought cancer survival would offer me a new lease on life. This wasn't always the case though.

For me though, it was more of a feeling of pressure to get my life back on track. Looking back now, I can tell this pressure was certainly irrational, but at the time, it felt very real. It was the impetus for some very bad decisions on who to spend my time with and efforts made to conform to what, at the time, I thought a "normal" person my age should be doing.

Long story short, I entered in a relationship with someone I was not compatible with because I thought it was time to get married and start a family. This ended up being one of the worst decisions of my life. It was followed by a divorce, a great sense of loss, and an addiction to gambling. Even before all of these challenges occurred, I knew I certainly didn't want to have to go through life-changing health scares in order to move towards the directions I wanted and desired. I also knew that I needed to find a way to move towards a path or purpose that was self-designed versus the constructs of conforming to societal norms. I also had this unshakeable feeling that while I succeeded immensely in finding a gift and purpose, initially with my health challenges, I failed miserably at maintaining the positive outcomes of this gift over the long-term. The possibilities for positive change, self-improvement, and success were abound after having the perspective of successfully navigating through the dirty, unstable, and personally unchartered muddy waters of cancer, yet within a year of my cancer diagnosis, I fell back into the metaphoric and, at times, personally deplorable box of everyday life.

Granted, there were other unforeseen challenges during this time – the unexpected loss of my mother, heartbreak, marriage and divorce, all within a short period after my initial cancer diagnosis. Despite this, I still felt as if I squandered away the unique gift and perspective of limitless positive motivation and related self-improvement by not keeping to my original zealous ambitions for never-ending positive personal change.

Sometimes, though, failure leads to insight. While I never created the perfect theory on how to create motivation upon demand, I did question myself as to why I wanted such motivation. I wanted results, or rather the emotional states associated with such results. After undergoing challenges, particularly my personal challenges such as the gambling struggles noted above, I became inspired to develop a framework for achieving positive results and this time maintaining them. This framework presupposed a certain amount of positive motivation, but such motivation was not the exclusive method to be utilized in creating the positive change desired. This framework was essentially the basis or foundational roots for this book. Certain distinctions were made during the process of drafting this book, including the realization that the desired results were secondary to the emotional states that were derived from such results. Additionally, I realized that the process of simply working towards such desired results could lead to higher emotional states. While I make no claims to have created the secret formula for on-demand motivation, I do claim to have crafted a framework, presented in this book, that will enable you to make the positive changes you want in your life, certainly not without effort, but rather in an authentic and gentle manner that will ensure your results are more than just transient moments in time.

When the initial drafting of this book was about 70 percent complete, I remember discussing a good deal of the premises and themes behind the book with my friend Natalie. While Natalie seemed to agree with a majority of the concepts that we discussed, related to the book, she noted that if she was looking to make a positive change, she would just read a book to get her motivated and pumped up. This made me really think about why I was writing this book and how this book distinguishes itself from many other books in the personal development field. The conclusion I came up with related to the unique value of this book is the fact that this book does more than provide mere motivation, but rather provides practical step-by-step instructions and an easy-to-follow framework for creating desired change and the corresponding results. My conversation with Natalie reminded me of the major frustration I have had with most personal development and self-help books. This frustration is that most of these types of books provide a good amount of short-term burst of motivation and interesting stories that tend to lead to short-term inspiration, but such books lack either a clear plan or outline for change that will last over both a short-term and long-term horizon. They also lack any type of explanation as to why the change method can be effective for you and in what contexts it should be applied. I have also encountered other books that tend to be overly technical and might provide insights for change, but such insights are buried between technical jargon and anecdotal rants.   Such books tend not to provide you with clear instructions on how to make lasting change as well as a background for the techniques for making such change without over-complication.

August 2016

"Yes!" exclaimed Josh with strong excitement.

I smile at him and tell him we are almost there. I have a

calm demeanor, but inside I'm excited yet nervous at the same time. Josh isn't quite as calm and reserved. We have an ever-increasing large crowd watching us. I am wondering why these people seem so obsessed with us and do not they have jobs or families to be with. Surprisingly, the crowd of onlookers are quite supportive, although there is an occasional "know it all" telling us what to do next. Josh quickly quirks back at him and tells him to mind his fucking business – not the most articulate way of getting his point across, but effective none the less. I can't say I blame him, when we are placing $600 bets a spin on roulette (on multiple spins), it's kind of our prerogative to choose our approach. For the most part, though, everyone is living vicariously through us, thrilled with our perceived "success." It's 3 PM on a steamy hot Wednesday afternoon. Location – just outside of Philadelphia city limits. We are playing video roulette at the local casino. We just had a huge win. We probably should have left. We definitely should have left- but we just couldn't.

After a long run, over months, of making a good deal of money, based on perceived repeat number patterns on these machines, we managed somehow to give all of our profits and then some back. Now we were on a mission to get back all the money we (or rather I) lost. We were close, so close we could smell, touch, and taste it. But we ultimately failed and failed miserably- just as every gambler will do in the long-run.

It didn't make any sense why we were even bothering with this. I guess this destructive behavior served as a distraction for me – a way to fill my time that recently had been very structured and accounted for, with very little free time to spare. I had recently gotten out of a really bad and unhealthy relationship. While this was certainly a long-term gain for me, I guess I viewed the end of the relationship as a short-term loss. This transient sense of loss was likely the trigger that sparked my need for distraction and avoidance.

Of course, there were other factors too that led to this addictive and non-productive behavior. A recent bout with cancer (as previously mentioned), other personal losses, and temporary career dissatisfaction were other underlying reasons that accounted for a perceived need for distraction through disempowering behaviors.

What made the least sense, though, was how shocking and hard these gambling losses hit me. While I was able to ultimately stop gambling before the financial losses destroyed me (as they do with most people), I certainly felt the financial hit and mental hit of such losses. When I spoke to my counselor/teacher about this, she posited that I was trying to build a buffer so I wouldn't have to work anymore – trying to avoid aspects of living or to trying to build a buffer to do something completely outside of my comfort zone (perhaps career-wise), and I was not worrying about financial losses associated with such risk. While it is subjective, we formulated that I placed too much of a correlation on my financial success to my happiness and satis-faction.

All of this made sense – but what should I do next? I should have known better and been able to easily snap back from the financial losses.   I mean, like I said, while it certainly is never fun to lose money, these losses initially wouldn't have a long-term impact on my life. Despite all of the logical examination I had done in relation to this subject, I was stuck. While this event seemed, at the time, to be a somewhat of an isolated episode, I spent several years going through similar circumstances, engaging in the same destructive gambling habits – winning money, losing more money, and wasting my time and potential. I felt little sense of meaning in my life, and I was left feeling like it was impossible to get that full sense of meaning back. It's not that I didn't want to. It's quite the opposite, actually. I would have given anything to get that full sense of meaning back, to feel I was at peace with myself, and to live life from a positive abundant mindset. I came up with a plan. Just let go of the past and move forward and build that meaning. Seems great, right? Seems logical, right?   It didn't work. Easier said than done, and no matter what I tried, I couldn't get out of this stuck state.

MY BACKGROUND

My name is Charlie. I have studied Neuro Linguistic Programming (NLP) for over fifteen years up to the master practitioner level. NLP is a psychological approach that involves analyzing strategies used by successful individuals and applying them to goal achievement. Results in NLP are typically achieved through examination and changes of perspective around subjective experience. I also have an MBA in management, augmented by a post-graduate certification in Organizational Psychology. I have worked primarily in the corporate business world but have had the opportunity to work with personal and corporate coaching clients, to help them improve their business and personal matters.

From my perspective, I do a good job of assisting and guiding my clients. I have helped my clients change in positive ways. Despite this, I couldn't seem to help myself get out of this feeling of being stuck, feeling like I had limited purpose in life, ruminating on my gambling losses, not seeing a personal sense of future – not feeling at peace with myself, as well as the on-going depression and anxiety at the time.   I applied various NLP techniques to myself to no avail.   All the techniques employed were, in my opinion, good, sound techniques.   I had used them in the past on myself and others, and they worked.   I stepped outside of my modality of NLP and tried techniques of applied positive psychology, time-line therapy, and human needs psychology, developed by Tony Robbins, as well as various aspects of spiritual techniques such as meditation, Human Design, GeneKeys, a general connection to the universe, and the law of attraction. While these approaches all seemed effective, logical, and useful, they didn't work for me at this particular time. I remember speaking with my best friend, Tom, about these challenges several times, and he kept telling me I needed to have more faith in God or whatever I believed in. Tom is very religious but in no way pushy. I tended to agree with him but again just couldn't seem to find a way to instantaneously find religion/spirit in my life. Despite my efforts, I wasn't a religious/spiritual person (at that time). I was stuck.

As I said, I had tried in the past to overcome these distraction-type behaviors using NLP techniques, but they didn't seem to work, for a variety of reasons. I enlisted the help of an outside counselor (non-NLP). While I felt this was beneficial for short-term coping strategies, there was so much of an emphasis on minor behavioral changes, as opposed to long-term lasting change, at the belief level. Ultimately, I knew this was a challenge that I had to work through on my terms.

Chapter 2

ORIGINS OF THE PROCESS

"Life runs on rhythms; life needs different things at different times"

Richard Rudd Author and Founder of the GeneKeys

What to do now?   I am not the type to give up (which contextually can be a great asset and at times can be a big liability, as you already can tell from the story I narrated related to my gambling challenges). I knew logically all the approaches I tried to deal with my challenges were tested, effective, and, for lack of a better word, were "good" approaches.   What if I was to combine these approaches, modify them slightly, change sequences, and add some subtleties, based on the principles I felt would exact lasting change for myself?

With this in mind, I experimented with this hybrid modification approach. I thought about the outcomes that I wanted most to reach. I analyzed these various techniques to determine what were the barriers in each technique that I previously tried on myself and how I could eliminate such barriers by either modifying the technique or adding a supplemental technique. I used the criteria of lasting positive change, inner clarity, a sense of purpose, a growth and contribution-focused future image, improved interpersonal relationships, feelings of connection (with self, others, and the universe as a whole), and generally a positive outlook with positive expectancy for the future and an overall improved self-concept in relation to the desired outcomes of the synthesis I was developing.

After days (which turned into months and years) of obsessive introspection, writing, more writing, experimenting, tweaking, testing, and re-testing, I developed the "Process." For a lack of a better term, I will simply refer to the method I developed as the "Process" in this book. I was happy with the product/framework, that I created, as I saw positive change from just the experimentation stage of *The Process*. Almost immediately after I saw the first signs of positive change, I thought I needed to share this, teach this, and put this out there for others so they can potentially benefit from using these techniques. I knew these tech-niques could help others in positive ways, as they have helped me.   That is where and when the concept of *The Process* was formally and originally derived from/created. Keeping in mind, by the time I came up with the ideas asso-ciated with *The Process*, I was at risk of taking a path of destroying my life through unhealthy behaviors.   Fortu-nately, things never got that far, but I strongly believe they would have headed in that direction and perhaps been led to disaster, had I not followed and implemented *The Process*.

Chapter 3

INTRODUCTION TO THE PROCESS

"Attitude is a choice. Happiness is a choice. Optimism is a choice. Kindness is a choice. Giving is a choice. Respect is a choice. Whatever choice you make makes you. Choose wisely."

Roy T. Bennett Author of The Light in the Heart

This book is a layman's guidebook – a "how-to" manual. You do not need to be a psychologist to read it, use it, and apply it. It is laid out in easy to follow steps to ensure your success. It should be read through in sequential order. As I mentioned above, sequence was a key component of setting up *The Process*. Sequence is integral to the success of applying *The Process* to yourself and creating the desired outcomes and changes you seek.

Please follow the exact sequence of this book.

DO NOT SKIP AHEAD.

With that said, I congratulate you for starting on the journey of making the changes you are about to make and the changes that you so deeply desire. *The Process* works. I know this because I have successfully used *The Process* on myself and helped others as well, utilizing *The Process*. You deserve to be happy. You deserve to feel purpose and meaning in your life. You deserve to know and be your authentic self. *The Process* will get you there in a gentle and minimally intrusive manner. There are many secondary gains or side benefits from employing *The Process*. Not only will you achieve your well-defined goals and feel and be more authentic, but you will also have an attitude and mindset of positivity, love, gratitude, and appreciation. This mindset will attract you to more positive situations, more positive relationships, and more positive interactions, which will, in turn, lead to the achievement of bigger goals than you ever imagined. Think of it this way – When you are struggling with a challenge or problem, you tend to have a victim mentality or negative mindset. This, in turn, tends to lead to more challenges and more problems. It can be a vicious cycle. For some people, this cycle seems to never end and/or continually pops up again and again in life. *The*

Process will reverse this vicious cycle and result in a cycle of achievement (on your own terms and based on how you define achievement) and positivity, which will lead to a stronger, more empowering mindset, which in turn will lead to more abundance and achievement.

General Concept Overview

The premise behind *The Process* is very simple – Positive thoughts and beliefs override or replace limiting thoughts and beliefs.   Said even simpler – A near-constant positive demeanor will lead to positive change. Again, this is the basic premise, and a lot more detail goes into *The Process* (including very detailed and specific instructions on how to execute it), but the starting point is a positive mindset.

I know this might sound especially challenging for those of you who are going through a challenging and depressive situation or for those who do not consider themselves opti-mists.   Please, though, remember what prompted me to write this book was a very challenging gambling addiction, divorce, and cancer recovery. My gambling losses were well over six figures. Being positive was not my first inclination, but it was something I knew I had to do and something that surprisingly became pretty organic with a little bit of prac-tice. Again, please trust me on this. Your positivity shift will be done in a gentle and easy way.

For some of you who are reading this book, your motivation is to improve on a currently satisfying situation, and you are inspired to take things to the next level. For others, you might be going through an extremely rough time and are desperate for change and help. *The Process* will help equally in both situations. It does not have to be adjusted or calibrated to your starting point.

Another key concept of *The Process* is damaging and less resourceful behaviors are replaced with positive, more resourceful choices and behaviors. One of the additional side benefits of working with *The Process* is that you will find more choices in your life than you ever thought available. In general, more choice and options as compared to less choice is a good thing that allows for more opportunity.

Most behavioral experts agree that a less-than-resourceful behavior simply cannot be eliminated by willpower alone; the less-than-resourceful behavior must be replaced with another behavior. *The Process* will allow you to replace your unwanted behaviors with more resourceful and positive behaviors. This is first accomplished by defining your ultimate desired outcome/behavior and regularly future-pacing (seeing, hearing, and feeling an event or result in a future context) this outcome through the use of journaling and writing. These writing exercises will allow you to put positive thoughts on paper and eliminate any written trail of negative or limiting beliefs, thoughts, and/or doubts. Eventually, in a short period of time, this positive outlook will generalize beyond just your conscious writing and will be present itself in your everyday thought process (at both a conscious and unconscious level). Your writings will be used as an accountability tool that propels you towards your goals and outcomes.

Because your writings are generally future-paced, meaning they take the perspective of the future when and while you are moving towards your goals, they will move your unconscious mind towards these goals. This will happen unconsciously and will even take place while you are sleeping. At this time, it is important to note that because you are utilizing your unconscious mind in a way that it has likely not been utilized in the past, you could possibly experience some unique temporary harmless side effects from utilizing *The Process*. These side effects are very minor and nothing to be concerned about. Sometimes, people will experience a sort of hazy or taxing feeling from a mental/psychological standpoint, upon waking up, during the first couple of weeks of implementing *The Process*. This typically happens when someone is moving away from a very challenging problem state or challenging situation. This can be best be described as sort of a feeling like your mind was working overtime while you were sleeping. Again, this does not typically occur with everyone. If you do feel like this, do not worry; this is only one indication that your subconscious mind is working for you in moving towards the solutions you desire.

As you undertake *The Process*, I will instruct you on

how to perform your journaling/writing in a fashion that also accentuates enjoying the steps along the way of you attaining goal-achievement/positive change. This is another key factor that makes *The Process* so successful. By enjoying the steps along the way of working towards your goals and desired outcomes, you will find fulfillment very early on in *The Process*. There are many ultimate outcomes of *The Process*, but perhaps the most crucial one is to live a life that contains a more pervasive sense of personal fulfillment.

Ultimately, the main goal of *The Process* is to develop a new replacement behavior that is aligned with your outcomes and goals and that is a resourceful and ecological behavior, but this is not always the case with behavioral change. For example, I worked with a client using *The Process* to overcome a smoking habit, which was a very non-resourceful addiction. Years prior to her addictive behavioral patterns associated with smoking, she was addicted to another non-resourceful behavior, unhealthy alcohol consumption, which led to detrimental effects in her personal and professional life. The reason she went from one destructive behavior to another was because she had not consciously replaced the destructive behavior with a positive replacement behavior. After several sessions working together and a good deal of individual work on her own (utilizing the steps in *The Process*), my client moved away from her destructive behaviors and replaced or overwrote them with behaviors that were enjoyable to her, congruent with her identity/values, and much more positive and ecological to her family system. These activities included professional development, tapping into her artistic side, and purposely and intentionally engaging in enjoyable activities such as gourmet cooking, art classes, as well as embracing her divine feminine side/energy. Note: See Chapter 5 for a discussion concerning ecology.

At this point, I would like to discuss NLP at a summary level, as a good number of techniques in *The Process* have foundational roots in NLP, and at the same time, it could appear as if I am also criticizing NLP for not being efficacious enough. I personally love NLP. I believe NLP is powerful. It is efficient and it is effective. NLP has changed my life immensely and contributed vastly in a positive fashion to the development of the person I have become. NLP has changed and improved countless lives for the positive across the world over the last forty years. In my experience, from interacting with a good number of doctorate-level psychologists in professional discussions, NLP is so much more effective than the standard treatment models that most psychologists and therapists are currently applying. It is much more efficient and effective than the majority of these models because *The Process* focuses on tangible ecological results. With that said, NLP is not a cure-all, and there are, in my opinion, certain change-acceleration methods and premises missing from most (not all) NLP's practitioner's toolbox.

The challenge, though, with the majority of these techniques, is two-fold. Firstly, it can be very difficult to self-execute such techniques without the assistance of a trained and competent NLP practitioner. Secondly, even with the assistance of a trained NLP practitioner, some people struggle to visualize. While the most proficient practitioner knows that all sensory inputs are valuable in utilizing change techniques, most tend to focus on visual techniques despite this. Consequently, when focusing on techniques, most NLP practitioners focus almost exclusively on visual techniques. *The Process* is based on the principle that change can occur on an individual level without external assistance in the form of a therapist, and one method for such change to occur is through the use of journaling and writing, which will eliminate roadblocks, such as visualization struggles and the need for a skilled practitioner to walk you through techniques in real-time.

At this point, it is important to make the differentiation between just goal achievement and what I would call "positive change," or more precisely, happiness. There is a multitude of books written about happiness. I remember in graduate school, we spent several classes discussing the construct of happiness in a management/leadership course. I will not spend too much time speaking about this concept other than to caution you that "success" and "goal-achievement" do not always equate to happiness.

It is important to set goals that align with your values, your higher purpose, and your identity. Several steps in *The Process* are specifically designed to congruently and accurately define your true sense of self at this identity level. Above and beyond that, though, I would recommend taking the approach of doing an internal evaluation of whether the goal/goals you choose to achieve using *The Process* will ultimately lead to a sense of fulfillment. The most accurate, precise, and concise summation of this concept (fulfillment) is something that I learned years ago from Anthony Robbins.   Tony developed the six human needs psychological approach, and he defines the last two human needs, the needs necessary for fulfillment, as growth and contribution. I encourage you to think about these two constructs when defining your goals that you will achieve using *The Process*. This means ensuring that your goal allows you to stretch and develop new skills, thought patterns, and behaviors that allow for long-term development and growth.   Secondly, but equally as important, you also want to make sure that your goal/goals allow you to go above and beyond just your personal needs and they allow you to contribute to others, whether those others be your family, local network, your community, or even the world in general.

The Process Notes:

The Process Notes:

Chapter 4

PILLARS OF THE PROCESS

"Do what makes you happy. If something doesn't make you happy then maybe you should rethink why you are doing it."

Beata Pokorny

---

1. Change occurs both at the conscious and subconscious level. The most powerful change occurs at the subconscious level, but change is necessary and will be enacted at both levels when utilizing *The Process*.

2. Think positive thoughts – *The Process* will train you to think positive thoughts. This will

profoundly change your mindset and your actions and thus the results you achieve.

3. *The Process* takes time, but not an excessive amount of time. In my experience, there is no such thing as major lightning-speed change that is meaningful. Conversely, change does not have to be the long, drawn-out, painful process that is favored by most contemporary psychologists and therapists.

4. Beliefs drive our decisions but changing or reframing limiting beliefs is not the only path to positive change. New positive beliefs can be installed without spending excessive time focusing on the old limiting belief or the old problem state. Such new belief systems will override past limiting beliefs unconsciously through *The Process*.

5. True happiness can only be achieved when you are your authentic self.

6. True happiness can only be achieved when you see yourself as a part of a bigger system.

7. Positive change can be done in a way that is gentle to the person and system (i.e. family system) experiencing such change.

The Process Notes:

Chapter 5

"No matter how small you start, start something that matters."

Brendon Burchard

---

1. By identifying your true authentic self and desires and goals, that are congruent with your identity, you can start to move towards those desires and goals – quickly.
2. Positive change will occur by programming your mind to see such positive change as already occurring – For some, this can be very challenging to do via visualization. *The Process*

employs different methods, not only visualization, for your conscious and unconscious mind to see such goal achievement, that will occur.

3. Each day you employ *The Process*, you are quickly building momentum towards achieving your goals and attaining true happiness. You will start to see and feel such changes both internally (feelings) and externally (results) in a very short period.

4. Negative self-talk and thoughts will naturally occur when you are in a problem state and/or attempting to create change. *The Process* does not attempt to fight such self-talk or negativity but rather simply acknowledges them and moves on. *The Process* employs a method that consciously avoids such negativity at specific times. Over a short time period, this method will generalize to the majority of your life – nearly effortlessly.

5. Limiting beliefs will be automatically and organically overwritten by more empowering beliefs.

6. Approach life from a place of abundance, love, empathy, positivity, and a caring mindset. This can be challenging at first, but again, this will be consciously performed during short periods and

will eventually generalize to a more pervasive, effortless, and unconscious state of mind.

7. Obstacles to happiness and goal achievement will be explored during *The Process*, but only briefly. The focus on *The Process* will be around identifying positive change and executing it through positive generative processes.

While these principles may seem daunting, they will be fully explained in detail in the chapters that follow. Examples of each of the major principles will be provided. Keep in mind, the presupposition behind *The Process* is that certain therapeutic techniques that did not work for you in the past in certain contexts were due to such techniques being too complex to apply to yourself or due to such techniques being overly theoretical and not practical. *The Process* attempts to limit such challenges so that they will not be present in the techniques presented in this book.

The Process Notes:

The Process Notes:

Chapter 6

Q&A AROUND THE PROCESS

"Don't be pushed around by the fears in your mind. Be led by the dreams in your heart."

Roy T. Bennett Author of The Light in the Heart

WHO WILL *THE PROCESS* HELP? / WHAT ARE THE POSSIBILITIES FOR *THE PROCESS*?

he Process can help a countless number of people, from those struggling with major life challenges to those attempting to make their life more positive. Challenges *The Process* can assist with include, but are not limited to, depression, anxiety, loneliness, certain addictions, motivational challenges, relationship challenges, and leadership challenges- just to name a few. The possibilities associated with *The Process* are endless. If you have a goal (any goal) you wish to achieve or want to feel more positive and authentic in your life, *The Process* will help you get there. *The Process* can be done individually or be done under the supervision of a counselor or therapist. I would even envision various self-help groups holding Process-type meetups to help build momentum and add accountability and a sense of community to *The Process*.

This book is not providing medical information, nor is it designed to diagnose, treat, or cure any medical disorders. You should seek advice from your medical professional for any and all current or potential medical issues/concerns.

WHAT IF I HAVE TROUBLE GETTING STARTED? HOW CAN I BE SURE THAT I WILL BE MOTIVATED TO MAINTAIN *THE PROCESS*?

Change, and more importantly, motivation for change, can be challenging at times. In my personal experience, people are more motivated by fear or pain than they are by rewards or potential pleasure. In actuality, we should take a dual approach and focus on both the positives of the change that you desire as well as the pain (both long-term and short-term) of not making the desired change you seek. While *The*

Process is pervasively designed to be gentle, it might be necessary for you to be introspective and contemplative and focus on what your life will look and feel like if you do not start to make the changes you desire immediately. Think in terms of how your life will look like, feel like, and generally how you will feel and how those important to you (family, friends, loved ones, etc.) will be impacted by you not making the changes you desire. While this step might be painful in the moment, it will help ensure you have the motivation to make your desired changes.

A personal story of mine, that is a perfect example of this type of motivation, is the cancer diagnosis I had several years ago. While this was a confusing time for me, with lots of conflicting advice from doctors, upon conclusion of my surgery, I ultimately choose to utilize a holistic treatment route instead of the doctor-recommended chemotherapy route. For me, this meant it was crucial that I act on the desired changes I wanted to make, which mostly included dietary changes and other therapeutic modalities. At this time, in this life-or-death context, motivation was automatic for me.

I made dietary changes that would have seemed impossible to me weeks before the cancer diagnosis. Anything that was a potential contributor to cancer returning was simply removed from my diet. Anything that was a potential deterrent to cancer was added to my diet. This included breaking a life-long habit of drinking over 60 ounces of soda per day, which was eliminated instantaneously. While this motivational surge was unique, as it was coded as a matter of life or death in my mind, it demonstrates how the power of 'away from' (avoiding pain) can be very useful in facilitating change.

If you are initially feeling unmotivated to start *The Process* or if you find yourself struggling to consistently implement *The Process*, it is recommended to take the point of view described above, related to the pain of not executing your desired changes. This should only be done briefly and not be written down. Just thinking about this a few times vividly will provide you with a surge of motivation to move forward towards the outcomes you desire. The main focus of *The Process* though is to focus on positive outcomes. That is why you should immediately follow up this mental exercise with either a written or mental exercise of projecting all the positive effects of the long, medium, and short-term, of the positive and resourceful changes you will make.

You should also remind yourself that *The Process* is a tested method, and if followed, it will work for you just as it has worked for me and others. You and your system (family, friends and loved ones) deserve the positive effects of the changes you have decided to make in your life by executing the steps in this book.

HOW LONG WILL IT TAKE TO SEE CHANGES FROM *THE PROCESS*?

Every goal is different in scope, so there is no set amount of time that can be used as a benchmark for the amount of time it will take for *The Process* "to work.' Generally, you will start to see both tangible results and a drastic change in your mindset after about 30 days (oftentimes much sooner). *The Process* is something that should be continually maintained throughout your life. After the first 30 days, the scope and frequency of the exercises can be trimmed down. This will be explained later in the book. Generally, behavioral change experts believe that lasting change will occur after 30 days of changing your habits.

As I previously stated, change is challenging. It is not easy to make impactful and lasting change. This is a good thing. If it were easy to make lasting and positive change, it would likely be as easy for us to slip into less resourceful states just as quickly, if not more quickly. In NLP, there is a saying that anything worth doing well is worth doing poorly at first. Change is a process, and if you follow *The Process*, the change you desire will manifest itself in a relatively short timeframe. One important piece of advice in relation to making the change process much gentler is to try to add as much structure to *The Process* as possible. There are certain steps in *The Process* that will automatically do this for you if they are followed, but if you try to apply this approach to all the steps of *The Process*, it will help make them a habit.

In his book, *The Power of Full Engagement*, Tony Schwartz speaks of the concept of habitualizing change or making change a periodic set habit. I strongly agree with this concept and encourage you to read *The Power of Full Engagement*.

It is also important to think about the context and scope of your problem state (change you want to make) in terms of timeframes. When we view problems from the lens of our own perspective, which is what most people tend to do, we can easily get overwhelmed by our problem state and default into inaction or paralysis. In order to avoid looking at your problem state only through the lens of your own perspective, *The Process* is set up in a manner in which the steps for change are automatically broken down into smaller steps. This is known as chunking. In terms of time, it is important for us to remember that while a challenge or problem state is certainly worthy of initiating immediate action and change to remedy or course-correct, it is also extremely important to remember that, as humans, we tend to see problems in terms of either the immediacy or the short-term consequences of such challenges. This too can lead to a state of inaction or paralysis preventing positive change. For this reason, *The Process* is structured to take a short, medium, and long-term view.

When approaching any challenge or important situation/decision, it is essential to view the challenge through the lens of multiple perspectives from a time and personal standpoint. For example, something that seems like a major problem to you in the moment might seem like a minor problem to someone else who knows you, because they can see the many other positives in your life in the current state you are in, as well as the many other positive potentialities in your future. This multiple perspective approach (time and personal viewpoint) will likely prevent inaction by making the problem state not so immediate. It will certainly not result in you dismissing the problem as a whole, as your first-person self-perspective will allow you to move towards achieving the positive change you seek. At this point, it is important to point out that when we are in a problem state, we tend to engage in what I call self-projected time distortions. We tend to believe that we will be stuck in this problem state, and the change we desire (or any change for that matter) will never happen. One of the main focuses of *The Process* is obviously to accelerate positive change, but there are times that change occurs organically even with a lack of a meaningful intervention. If you find yourself hesitating to start *The Process* because you have a self-projected time distortion of change taking too long, you should immediately do two things. Firstly, look inward and find several counterexamples of times in which major change took place in your life over relatively short periods of time (think in terms of a year to several years), with very little conscious change work being performed on your part. You will be shocked to realize that so much change took place in your life over short periods of time. This awareness of past organic change will help add a new perspective on how easy change can be for you. Once you have already come to the conclusion that change is more prevalent and naturally occurring than you previously thought, combine this thought with the fact that *The Process* is a change-oriented system that has worked for many people with similar challenges to yours. This new perspective will allow you to realize that the positive changes and new outcomes you seek can be easily and systematically attained by applying *The Process*.

Another key point to examine when performing any type of change work is are you, as the person who is executing the change work, in the right mindset to be making such changes? Oftentimes we will have overlapping or competing priorities from our past experiences which limit our ability to have clarity throughout the change process. What is needed to overcome this potential limitation is something I refer to as a "psychological reset." This term refers to the blank mental slate which will allow you to establish goals strictly on a stand-alone basis and not in terms of compensations related to failed past endeavors.

An example of a time in which a psychological reset is needed and is essential is the start of a new relationship. You must come to the start of a new relationship with a lack of broad generalizations and projections from past relationships or you will not be able to fully see and feel what is present in front of you at the current time, in your new relationship. If you fail to approach the new relationship without the benefits of a psychological reset, you will be inserting generalizations, fears, and other uncertainties from a past timeline into your current timeline that do not relate to your current relationship partner. Another example of the need for a psychological reset could be in terms of financial or business endeavors. If you approach a goal, such as starting a new business, with an underlying motive of making up for a past financial loss/business failures, you will be compromising the wholeness of the new businesses success by using outdated metrics (making up for past losses/failures) instead of utilizing the contextually appropriate metrics that are relevant for your new business. It is important that you enter in your new goal achievement undertaking with the clarity of a stand-alone basis. This allows you to be focused on that new goal and the related steps need to attain it.

The Process Notes:

The Process Notes:

The Process Notes:

The Process Notes:

Chapter 7

STEPS IN THE PROCESS

"Most human beings don't design their lives intelligently- Most human beings don't design their lives at all. You have to design your life and that takes self-discipline; it takes care. You have to be thoughtful."

Richard Rudd - Author of and Founder of the GeneKeys

NOTE – THESE STEPS WILL BE DISCUSSED IN FURTHER DETAIL WITH TANGIBLE EXAMPLES IN SUBSEQUENT CHAPTERS WITHIN THIS BOOK.

WEEK 1 - ONE-TIME STEPS

1. Identify your ideal life, in tangible terms, over the next six to twelve months. Write down what your life looks and feels like, at that time, with no limitations or obstacles. Don't think about this step; just write down what comes to you from your subconscious mind. Think in terms of health, career, finances, relationships, achievements, self-concept (positive) spirituality, your environment (house, living situation etc.), confidence, or any other relevant construct or value that is personally important.

2. Define your authentic identity. This identity must be aligned and be congruent with your core values and beliefs. Write this down as well. Again, this will be discussed in further detail later in this book.

3. Consciously identify parts or obstacles that might be unintentionally directing you away from your goals and life that you desire.

4. Develop a mental visual representation of your ideal self that is based on the results of performing steps (1) and (2) above. This representation will be used as an anchor to

overcome past obstacles and remove them from the future.

ONGOING STEPS (STARTED IN WEEK 2)

1. Review items from Week 1 – Step 1, noted above, on a daily basis (THIS CAN'T BE UNDERESTIMATED, as this is foundational in your new mindset programming).
2. In a journal or in the spaces provided in this book, write a detailed description of a day in your life 30 days from now. This writing should be in 1st person and takes the perspective of you having successfully worked towards your goals during the last 30 days. It is written from a place of positivity, gratitude, and confidence. This writing will be redrafted periodically.
3. Each night, just before you go to bed, read the latest version of what was written in step (2) above under ONGOING STEPS and attempt to visualize yourself from an associated perspective. (Associated here means 'seeing things as if the event were actually happening.') If you have difficulty visualizing this, that is not a problem. This will be addressed in step 4 below.
4. When you are finished visualizing or attempting

to visualize as described in (3), turn inwards and ask your subconscious mind to work for you while you are sleeping to process and move towards the attainment of the activities and goals described in (2) above and your image described in (3) above. Your subconscious mind always wants to be aligned with your true self and all your wants and desires. It will gladly work to help you move towards your goals while you sleep.

5. Each day in the morning, write an abbreviated description of all you will have accomplished during that day that is aligned with positivity, love, inner peace and moving your goal achievement noted in (2). Note the perspective through which this will be written will be after the day is over. You are training your mind to see the reality of your daily goals and move towards them.

6. At the end of each day, review your daily writing from (5) and make note of what you accomplished that day from your writing. Do not be self-critical here. Set your intention to learn from what you have and have not accomplished. Be sure to make note of the positive behaviors, interactions, and actions that took place during the day that you might not have even written

down when you were originally framing out your day.

7. Every time a negative thought comes to mind, simply acknowledge it and do not dwell on it. If it was a thought of a previous regret you had, simply acknowledge to yourself that it happened, and you have accepted it and learned from it. This is very important. You are training your brain to not dwell on negativity. This, combined with the positivity from all your writings, is literally rewiring your brain to move towards a more loving, positive, and grateful mindset that is long-lasting and organic.

WHAT IF YOU DON'T WANT TO REPLACE AN OLD BEHAVIOR, BUT RATHER JUST INSTALL A NEW WANTED BEHAVIOR?

People who are ultimately seeking out pleasure will find spontaneously that through the use of the old behaviors that were even mildly less-than-resourceful will disappear or be lessened to a greater extent (i.e. over-eating, excessive anger, unhealthy eating, and other less than optimal health and communication habits).

HOW IS POSITIVE THINKING INCORPORATED INTO *THE PROCESS*?

The Process also incorporates a constant positive outlook through the use of filters available through the act of writing items related to your change initiative. When you write something, you have complete control over what makes it to the paper. Visualization, conversational, and other thought processes sometimes bring up negative topics or less empowering pictures and sounds that we cannot consciously control.

By focusing on writing at the initial steps in *The Process*, you can:

1. Focus easily on filtering out all non-positive thoughts. No negative thoughts will be expressed in your journaling and writing, which will generalize your mind towards a more positive outlook.

2. Engage more lasting change through the higher activation of your reticular activating system, or "RAS." Without complicating things, at a basic level, RAS is a part of your brain that deciphers what is important and more easily retained.

3. Incorporate items that are essential for change but are difficult to visualize initially, such as the expression of positive experiences that will over-

power/over-write previously less resourceful experiences. These experiences will take place from the standpoint of having already occurred, which will move your brain towards positive expectancy. These experiences will also take the format of being enjoyed during the process of change, and an overall positive outlook will be incorporated into these writings. These are processes that are very challenging to do when in a non-resourceful state and utilizing only visualizations or sensory constructions.

4. Create future-paced experiences more fully. Such positive experiences will create both immediate and lasting enjoyment and change.

5. Keep tangible track of the progress in your writing.

6. Have readily accessible positive states available to you through the reading of your journaling.

7. Enable more powerful visualizations (if necessary), as written experiences will be much easier to visualize after the process of journaling them has taken place.

The Process Notes:

The Process Notes:

The Process Notes:

The Process Notes:

"If you don't thoughtfully design your life, you will be victim of the status quo or quite possibly worse...much much worse."

Charlie Minanno

WEEK 1- DAY 1

Welcome to Week 1-Day 1 of *The Process*! The steps you take in Week 1 will lay down the foundation for *The Process*. Week 1 will be challenging and introspective. You will feel a strong sense of alignment and wholeness after just one day of exercises.

In full disclosure, Week 1 – Day 1 will be the most time-consuming of all days, but it will be well worth the time you put in. The time and effort you put in on Day 1 will pay huge dividends for you in a short period of time; for some people the positive results are seen and felt almost immediately.

WEEK 1-DAY 1

<u>Step 1</u>

- Identify your ideal life in tangible terms over the next six to twelve months.
- Write them down – no limitations or obstacles. Don't overthink this; just write down what comes to you from subconscious mind.
- Think in terms of health, career, finances, relationships, achievements, self-concept (positive) spirituality, and environment (house, living situation, etc.), and confidence.

In order to create the positive change in your life, you will have to clearly define what you want in tangible terms. By writing down your vision for your ideal life (i.e. what you want) over the next six to twelve months, you will move your subconscious mind in that direction. Also, as stated above, at a very basic level, you cannot get to where you want unless you have a destination in mind. That is why it is important to be very detailed and precise in journaling out your ideal life six to twelve months from now. Because you have the benefit of filtering out what makes it to the paper, it is essential that you only list items that are stated in positive terms. DO NOT write what you don't want – You have to think in positive tangible terms.

When you are writing out your ideal life, think in terms of positive expectancy and from a viewpoint of enjoying the process of meeting these goals. As I mentioned in the introductory chapters, there can be a difference between goal achievement and happiness. You ideally want to think in terms of both. Remember the most fulfilling goals are those in which we are growing and developing, as well as contributing to others. I know these guidelines might seem a bit overwhelming, especially since I noted not to overthink this process, but the guidelines are important and are there to keep you alert to the outcomes you want. There will be a time to briefly proof and edit this exercise when you are done, so do your best – as long as it comes from your heart it will work in creating what you desire. Below is an example of my Week 1-Day 1/Step 1 writings, from before this book was written, that will serve as a great example/framework to start with. Below is a section to fill in with your writings. Remember, there is no time limit on this – just don't overthink it and go with your heart.

WEEK 1- DAY 1

Example- <u>MY IDEAL LIFE IN 6 to 12 MONTHS</u>

- Published Author – 2 to 3 books
- $XXX,XXX in annual consulting income
- Animal Advocacy service at least twice a month
- Deep connection with nature and spending time in nature at least three times a week
- Dramatic improvement and rapid advancement in NLP skill attainment and utilization
- $XXX,XXX in net worth
- Deep connection with a pet – knowing that I provide him/her the most possible love, attention, and gratitude possible
- Loving relationship that is very open in emotional communication, intimacy, sexuality and partnership, and common goals and common values of making a contribution and difference in the world
- Fifteen personal coaching clients per month (outside of existing coaching work I do in a corporate consulting environment)
- Continued emotional and mentorship of children who are in my life (i.e. my Goddaughter Elianna)
- Continued deep connection with my immediate family – being able to better understand their

needs and meet them in a way that provides a
vehicle for them to feel loved and appreciated

- Rapid advancement in my martial arts class –
attaining a feeling and a sense of mastery in
the arts
- Teacher of NLP Practitioner Class
- Coaching a fairly competitive youth/junior high
basketball team
- Steady financial contributions to charities I care
about
- Contributing as an active board member of a non-
profit
- A highly organized household/environment and
lifestyle (structure and habit)
- Being recognized as a subject matter expert in the
Organizational Psychology (OD) field and
because of this, being a regular expert
speaker/panelist as various OD/HR events
- Cooking various healthy and delicious vegan
meals at least 3 times a week
- A YouTube channel or podcast based on various
topics that are important me
- Teaching classes at a university level (number of
classes depends on client-load/time commitment)

COMMENTS ON MY IDEAL LIFE WRITING

Before you begin writing, there are a couple items that are noteworthy from my example exercise. Firstly, as you review my goals, notice how they are all mostly within my control. Of course, there are always going to be external factors that potentially impact your goals, but as you can see, the majority of the variables that influence my goals are within my control. Also, as you carefully read my example goals, you can see the specificity of my goals/outcomes. Without a clear representation of what you want, there is very little chance of you identifying the means of getting there. That is why for the most part, they are not general constructs like happiness, love, being fit and healthy, or confidence. While these constructs are definitely important to me and, generally speaking, important to most of us, they are presupposed in my goals. For example, my goals of achieving mastery in martial arts and healthy cooking presuppose health. My goal of public speaking presupposes confidence. My detailed goal of an intimate relationship presupposes love. It is essential that we initially work with details that are very specific and tangible so that we program our subconscious mind to work towards these goals with clarity and specificity. Do not worry – we can and will adjust the specifics of these goals as time passes, circumstances change (as with life in general), and more self-clarity is attained. Another underlying principle of NLP is behavioral flexibility, and we will certainly exercise a good amount of behavioral flexibility in revisiting and revising our goals during the Process.

It is important to also note though that while specificity is always desired in our goal-setting exercise (and with goal-setting in general), there are some circumstances in which we simply do not have enough information to generate a very specific goal. This should not preclude the goal, as this goal assuredly came from your heart and is important to you. As you move further along with the Process, more information will come to light, and a greater-level specificity can be layered onto this goal.

A perfect example of this for me was my goal of finding a deeper spiritual meaning in life. At the time of writing that goal, all the information I had available was only that I had an interest in learning more about my spiritual path. It was something that was lacking in my life and something I had a desire for, so the lack of information that would lead to specificity was to be expected. As I find my spiritual path, a more specific goal will be generated.

Additionally, it is important to note that while this is a goal-setting exercise, the items on your list are not static; they are on-going processes. For example, my list contained items/interactions/achievements that I did not have when I wrote the list, but that doesn't mean simply attaining those items is a completion point. There were many steps involved in reaching these goals.

Another step in the Process will focus on achieving your goals and ensuring that such process is enjoyable and not burdensome. For now, though, it is important to note your outcomes and your ideal life and realize that some of these items will be tangible goals, some might be on-going activities, and some outcomes may also be processes or the maintenance of processes that were previously set in motion. The bottom line is that your list should represent a state of pure enjoyment, fulfillment, and satisfaction in your life. There should be no limitations when writing your goals/ideal life other than restriction of ensuring the goals are mostly within your control, as previously noted, and also that the goals are ecological (see subsequent paragraph related to ecology).

Lastly, when you are done writing your goals, you should perform what NLP calls an ecology check. This is ensuring that there are no negative unintended consequences of your goals (to yourself and others). A perfect example of this would be an ambitious young yoga studio owner who might choose the goal of opening up three more yoga studios and juice bars within the next year. While on a stand-alone basis this might seem like a very good ambitious goal, when an ecology check is performed, it would very evident that the same yoga studio owner is also the mother of two young children and her family system would likely be very adversely affected and disrupted by attempting to achieve such time-consuming goals. An ecology check would allow her to define and work towards a goal that was more balanced and avoid costly unintended consequences, while still achieving the success she desired in a much more balanced and ecological fashion.

MY IDEAL LIFE IN 6 to 12 MONTHS WOULD LOOK AND FEEL LIKE

The Process Notes:

The Process Notes:

The Process Notes:

The Process Notes:

WEEK 1- STEP 2

Define Your Authentic Identity

Now that you have formulated your ideal life in the short-term to medium-term in WEEK 1 – Step 1, it is time to identify your true self – your identity, your core values, and beliefs. You must ask yourself the age-old question: "Who am I?" The answer to this question isn't about being a lawyer, a doctor, a mechanic, or whatever your profession of choice is, but rather who you are at your core. Think in terms of permanency and not transient traits. Use past reference points in your life where your true character really was tested and stood out to help shape who you are now. The answer to this very deep and meaningful question of "Who am I?" should encompass your deepest values and beliefs about yourself, the world, and life in general. Virtually every spiritual practice seeks an answer to this question. Regardless of the differences amongst these religious or spiritual practices, they all revolve back to this identity-level question.

Defining and designing your ideal self-image is an essential foundation in the Process. A positive sense of identity and self-concept will gravitate you towards the change you desire and the goals you will achieve. It will also ensure the changes and goals you desire are congruent or aligned with your core identity.

At this point, you might be thinking, "Wouldn't it be more efficient to first detail my true self/identity and then formulate my ideal life?" While this is one approach, the Process opts to first detail your ideal life, as this is coming from your heart and subconscious and it is presupposed in detailing your ideal life that your true-self/true-identity will shine through in your DAY 1 –Step 1 exercise. To better explain this, generally speaking, you are not formulating or developing your authentic identity – your authentic self is already within you. You are simply transferring this concept from your thought processes to paper. While it is always admirable and, at times, essential to aspire to change your core values and beliefs surrounding your identity, the Process works by recognizing the many positive constructs that define who you are now as a person. There certainly are other techniques that utilize refining your self-concept or what you identify as your self-concept. The techniques are also very effective but, in my experience, very challenging to execute on your own and generally need the guidance of an experienced practitioner. The Process allows you to gently appreciate the many positive qualities that you iden-tify as being core to who you are and to work with these core qualities to ensure your goals and ideal life are congruent with your current identity.

My top core values that define me personally are intro-spective, outside-the-box thinker, caring, compassionate, dedicated (never giving up on something I believe in), empathetic, vegan, and family/friend-oriented/helper.

When I was in the brainstorming process of developing these core values, I felt a bit stuck. One by one, I thought back to past reference points in my life that really defined me. My biggest reference points that helped provide extreme clarity were my healing from cancer, supporting my mother, and not giving up on her when the doctors told me she had 48 hours to live (she lived an additional two years beyond this diagnosis), caring for my father when he had cancer, adopting and caring for my dogs (Bowser and Woody) who were both in a tough spot before I adopted them, and choosing to live a vegan lifestyle.

When I was diagnosed with testicular cancer in 2013, it was a shock. I quickly had surgery, the tumor was removed, and I was informed that cancer had not spread. Multiple doctors told me I absolutely needed "preventative" chemotherapy just to be safe and certain the cancer would not spread. This didn't make sense to me. This is where my core values of critical thinking/introspection, dedication, and outside-the-box thinking became essential. I explored more empowering health options. I learned as much as I could about the dietary benefits of a raw vegan diet. I ate and drank things I couldn't have imagined eating or drinking a year earlier (even though I was already a vegan at that time). I studied the psychological factors, namely beliefs systems, and their impact on cancer and health. These are examples of how thinking about one reference point event allowed me to elicit many of the constructs of my true self. I won't go into further details of the events mentioned above because I am sure you can understand at this point how those events would help elicit core values. Remember using reference points that are relevant to your own life will help you to elicit the components of your true self.

When journaling your true identity, be sure to utilize only positive descriptors of your identity. As mentioned in the introduction to this book, one of the pillars of the Process is to approach the steps in the Process (and life in general) with a very positive frame of mind. I worked with a client once, and after giving her this assignment, I noticed that while she had many positive descriptors for her identity, she also had many less than resourceful descriptors. We want to avoid this. One of the major benefits of the Process is we can filter out into writing all negatives and only focus on positive items. That will allow us to move closer to our goals and build momentum over a relatively short period of time. This aspect of the Process will soon allow our unconscious minds to generalize this thought process so that it happens automatically, leading to even more positive thinking and optimism, which, in turn, will lead to an even greater level of success with the attainment of our goals.

While in Week 1-Step 1, I cautioned you not to overthink your journaling and writing. During Week 1 –Step 2, you should take your time and be very thorough and introspective with this. There is a greater level of precision that is required for this second exercise versus the first. Said differently, your goals can be much more malleable over time so there is room for adjustment. Your true self and identity are much less malleable. Yes, your identity can and will certainly change over time, but for the most part, it is much more static and fixed, compared to your goals and aspirations. This is a good thing. It ensures that, for the most part, your authentic self will shine through, even in tough times of challenge and uncertainty.

Below is my complete sample WEEK 1 – Step 2 Journal Writings, as well as an area to journal your own writings.

WEEK 1 - STEP 2

EXAMPLE – <u>MY TRUE SELF – "WHO AM I?"</u>

At my core, I am vegan. Not matter what changes in my life, I will always be a vegan because no other behavior or lifestyle will encompass my core values of compassion, empathy, equality, and minimizing suffering. I am animal lover and am extremely caring and compassionate caretaker for the world's most distinguished dog, Lord Bower (whose has sadly since passed from this realm of existence at the time of the writing).

I am a loving brother and son, and my family looks up to me. They know that I would do anything for them. I am a natural problem-solver and have a very unique outside-the-box approach. I am naturally a people-helper, and I am dedicated to helping others, whether it be through my professional endeavors or my personal interactions. I am very generous and try to help others as much as I can. I try to understand where people are coming from so I can better relate to them and, in turn, help them and be there for them when they need me. I am emotionally open, and I bring this openness to my relationships in a positive manner. I am loving and will do anything for my loved ones. I am a dedicated hard-worker and a life-time learner. I am realistic and evaluative with myself. I am committed to my development and growth. I am trusted by others and viewed as a trusted advisor. I am extremely dedicated, and when I believe in something or someone strongly enough, I will do whatever it takes to follow it through to completion. I am a caring and giving person. I always look to help out people who are in need and genuinely care about the best interest of everyone I interact with.

When I first started drafting the description above, it was challenging. What worked for me and has also worked for people I have helped is to start off drafting your description of your authentic self and true identity in bullet-point format. This will allow you to have several key concepts that are not constrained or restricted to being more than a couple key phrases. From there, you should review your bullet points and put them in a paragraph format that flows. This will allow your identity to feel more tangible, and it will also give you the feeling of being actively connected to your authentic identity instead of just reciting it.

Most corporations have a mission, vision, or even ambition statement that they utilize. The companies that I have worked with that actually live and breathe their mission, vision, and ambition tend to have the most congruent culture, least amount of conflict, and the most aligned workforce. This is because these companies have a vision and mission that is aligned with the values and beliefs of the organization. You should think of your authentic identity writing to be a sort of indirect personal mission or vision statement. A written form of how your values and beliefs shape your perspective of who are, at your core, as a person. When you review this writing exercise, do not just read it passively or intellectually. See and feel it from an emotional framework that triggers strong positive emotions about the many positives you have at your core.

As humans, we tend to have a distorted view of reality. This includes less than resourceful distortions about who we are as a person. We tend to see our life situation, as well as our self-concept, through a much more critical lens than others perceive it. While this might be helpful in the context of self-motivation at any given time, it can also be damaging because our self-concept or self-identity will drive our perceptions, which, in turn, will drive our decision and actions. Invariably we, as humans, tend to look at other people and only see the positives in such people's lives, while filtering out the invariable challenges, limitations, and disappointments in other people's realities. What is interesting is we actually tend to over-emphasize the limitations that we face personally, while filtering out the many positives, both characteristics and circumstances, that are present in our own lives.

To help overcome the distortion bias that could occur during this exercise, I suggest you not only take the perspective of yourself when defining your authentic self, but also the perspective of others, specifically loved ones, friends, colleagues, etc., who understand and appreciate your many positive characteristics. Whenever we have to examine something that is of importance, it is essential to examine things from multiple perspectives, not only yours, but that of others, both those who would also be impacted by your evaluation and those who could look at situation from an objective, unbiased perspective. This will allow for more relevant and useful information to be presented and evaluated, thus leading to more choices and ideas around your self-identity.

When you have completed your drafting of your authentic self/true identity, you should then do a quick congruency check of your identity with your ideal life six to twelve months from now, your Week 1 -Step 1 exercise. You should ensure that the goals you listed and the ideal life you can picture six to twelve months from now are aligned with your portrayal of your authentic self. For example, if your authentic self has a subset of values that revolve around being caring and being a people-helper and your six to twelve months goals revolve primarily around financial gains, then there is probably a mismatch there. If you find mismatches or a lack of alignment between your goals and identity, you should re-evaluate your goals. Your identity should be primarily fixed and is much less malleable than your goals. You want your identity to certainly evolve over time, but it should be the most foundational aspect of your life. True happiness and fulfillment will be attained through engaging in activities that are aligned and congruent with your values and your identity. If you feel like you are being your authentic self, while attaining goals and success that are aligned with your authentic self, your happiness and fulfillment will be above and beyond anything you could imagine right now.

DESCRIPTION OF MY AUTHENTIC SELF

The Process Notes:

The Process Notes:

The Process Notes:

WEEK 1 - STEP 3

Consciously identify parts or obstacles that might be unintentionally directing you away from your goals.

Often, our motivation towards a positive goal fails due to a lack of motivation. This often happens when we are in a stuck state or behavioral pattern for a certain amount of time and reach an internal frustration point. It can also occur when the universe gives us a surprise outside of our control (i.e. health challenges or another unexpected challenge). Other times, positive change can be initiated by simply feeling stuck in the status quo for a period of time, knowing that there is more out there for you to do, feel, and accomplish. These again are all what I describe as 'away from' motivation or moving away from an unwanted state, behavior, or circumstance.

The other type of motivation, 'towards motivation', is simply moving towards a positive outcome or circumstance which you desire. Most self-development professionals will speak in terms of motivation being either towards or away from motivation. I disagree on this point, as I do not believe that the motivational styles are always mutually exclusive. I believe that most situations are tilted towards either towards or away from motivation, but most of the time there are components of both motivational directions in what is driving a person from a motivational standpoint. I believe this is much more prevalent in terms of towards motivation. I say this because in my experience, both with people that I have helped and my personal experience, anytime someone is moving towards a positive goal or outcome, there is at least one state or behavior they are simultaneously motivated to move away from. While I believe this is presupposed in most NLP texts, I posit that such away from motivation as a sub-component of towards motivation is powerful enough in most cases that it should also be addressed and not just dismissed. It is also my experience that the majority of change is the result of a dominant away from motivation. As stated in the introduction to this book, one of the fundamental pillars of the Process is that you cannot simply move away from something (a behavior or state) without replacing it with a more resourceful behavior or state.

In virtually any type of change that results in a lasting resourceful behavior, a less-than-resourceful behavior is typically eliminated. This is not always done consciously, but nonetheless, there is an elimination or decrease in a less than resourceful behavior that takes place. While the majority of the Process is built around gently focusing on what you want, there is one step in the Process that examines previously occurring and less than resourceful behaviors and allow you to better understand and come to terms with such unresourceful behaviors. This technique is a hybrid version of the traditional six-step reframe in NLP. This is the most technical writing you will perform in the Process, and I have intentionally made it very gentle and not overly technical to work through, without sacrificing the efficacy of the technique.

The basis behind the traditional six-step NLP part reframe is finding the positive intent of the part of you that is responsible for engaging in a less than resourceful behavior; recognizing the part's positive intention; celebrating, thanking and acknowledging this part for its' positive intention; and working with this part to more resourcefully reach the outcome or positive intent originally desired. This technique is generally most effective when performed under the guidance of a skilled NLP practitioner. This is because the primary means of communication for this process is communication at a subconscious level. It is a difficult technique to execute without a guide or practitioner, as there can be a great deal of confusion as to where you are in the technique (i.e. Are you in the part, the guide, etc.?).

Our Week 1- Step 3 exercise involves performing the majority of a six-step reframe but doing so consciously through journaling and then rereading your journaling and asking your subconscious mind to process such information. Despite its change in format, this exercise will still allow you to recognize the positive intention of your unwanted behaviors, thus allowing you to move forward more easily with achieving your desired change/outcome. This part of the Process will also allow you to see the gift in the sufferings and challenges resulting from your unwanted behaviors.

In addition to these positive outcomes, this exercise will provide with you more choices in your behavioral repertoire. This is actually one of the most beneficial outcomes of the Process. It should be emphasized that while ultimately the goal of the Process is for you to achieve the positive outcomes and goals that your desire and that are aligned with your authentic self, this can only happen by adding more choices to your current framework from which you operate. Below details the steps we will use in this part of the Process:

1. Identify your unwanted behavior.
2. Put yourself in the perspective of this behavior. Use scratch paper to write down different thoughts that come to your mind that explain the positive intention of this unwanted behavior. An example of this would be the positive intention behind the part of a person responsible for smoking could be to interact with other smokers. Whatever positive intention comes to mind, write it down, but then chunk this positive intention up to a higher level. For example, the positive intention associated with interacting with other smokers could be chunked up to being included and relating to others – a sense of belonging. Chunking up to higher level would include feeling at peace with oneself. The higher you

chunk something up, the more abstract the result is. (i.e. feeling safe, feeling secure and okay). Similar to Week 1- Step 1, it is important not to overthink this aspect of the Process; just be in a relaxed state with an open mind and allow your unconscious to speak to you.

3. Give this part a name - the first name that comes to mind is fine (or the second one if the first one doesn't really track with you). Again, let your unconscious mind come up with this part's name and don't overthink it.

4. Draft a letter to the part that is responsible for executing this unwanted behavior. In this letter, you are to apologize to this part (by name) for not recognizing it and its positive intention earlier. Express your sincere gratitude to this part for trying to do something positive for you. Explain to this part that you will always be willing to listen to it, and there will be times in the future you might call on it for this behavior, but at this time you will be exploring other behavioral options, and the part is going to get a long overdue break/vacation. Let the part know that you too want the same positive intent that it wants, and you are beginning a process of working diligently to get that positive intent utilizing some other parts of you. Let that part

again know how grateful you are for it trying so hard to achieve its positive intent and let it know that it will always be with you, and you will periodically check in with it and let it know about the progress you are making in achieving the part's positive intent.

Once this letter is written, retain and reread it periodically. By periodically, I mean when you feel this contextually less than resourceful behavior tempting you or overwhelming you. This will serve to reinforce the original intent you had as it relates to your past unwanted behaviors. This will also allow you to forgive yourself and "go easier" on yourself for these past behaviors. It is important to note that while these past behaviors might have led to past suffering for you, they also provided you a gift- an avenue to greater clarity towards your goals and a new empowering future. You should read this letter at least one time after you write it – preferably before bed and ask your unconscious mind to process the information in this letter.

Even if from your perspective, your goals are solely being motivated by moving towards a positive goal and not moving away from an unwanted behavior, you can still benefit from using this part of the Process. You simply should think about what behaviors might be eliminated when you reach your goals. A very simple example of this might be moving towards greater health. You might have, in the past, spent time in avoidant behavior such as watching TV or over-eating and thus that you should examine the positive intent of such behavior. In this example, the behavior and part responsible for the behavior of over-eating or indulgent TV watching would be the part that is worked with.

POSITIVE INTENTION WRITTEN PART REFRAME WRITING

The Process Notes:

The Process Notes:

The Process Notes:

The Process Notes:

One final thought on your Week 1 writing exercises is that they can be split into multiple timeframes. I would also recommend not trying to do all these steps in one day. As stated earlier, these are exercises will be the most fulfilling and meaningful and at the same time the most introspective and challenging. It is perfectly okay if you have to chunk these exercises down to several days' worth of writing that spans more than one week. One of the pillars of the Process is to provide for positive change in the gentlest way possible. If you are feeling like this is too much writing for one week, pick up where you left off on the following week. The only piece of advice I would give you would be to finish whatever particular exercise you are on in one sitting, if possible. This is to ensure continuity, cohesion, and positive utilization momentum. Essentially you are doing three very powerful, challenging, and introspective writings in the Week 1 exercises. If you want to break these down into two weeks, that is fine, but I would not go beyond two weeks, or you will lose momentum. I had one client who did these Week 1 writings over the course of two days. That is what worked for her, and she was able to make some powerful changes in a very short period of time. Just go with the timing and pace that works best for you.

WEEK 1 - STEP 4

Develop a Visual Representation of Yourself - (Non-Writing Exercise)

You have already done tons of work here! This last Week One step is optional but encouraged. After performing the other steps in Week One, you likely have developed an organic image of your future self that is already living in alignment with your deepest goals and values and is also actively working towards your ideal dream life. I would recommend creating a picture and even a feeling of what this future self looks like now and briefly recreating this representation on a daily basis when you feel both empowered and challenged. Again, this will serve to both anchor and propel you towards where you want to be.

General Notes about Week 1

One last item to keep in mind is how to utilize all the work that you did during Week 1 of the Process. To sum it up briefly: Try to read it and feel it as much as possible. I certainly recommend that this should be done before bed, but I would also reread these during the week, again in times of both empowerment and challenge. This will help keep you on the path. When in doubt, reread and try to internally feel and view the contents of your Week 1 writing.

The Process Notes:

The Process Notes:

The Process Notes:

Chapter 9

"We need 4 hugs a day for survival. We need 8 hugs a day for maintenance. We need 12 hugs a day for growth."

Virginia Satir - Legendary Therapist

Congratulations! You have completed the most challenging yet rewarding, fulfilling piece of the Process!

At this point, you now have clarity on how you define yourself as a person (your character, your strengths, your values), what your ideal life looks like, from a medium-term standpoint and also what has potentially held you back from achieving your goals in the past. As discussed in the intro-duction to this book, clarity and specificity are key elements to achieving the outcomes you desire.

In my estimation, you now have more clarity on what you want and who you are as a person than roughly 95% of the people in the world. It is very important that you take the time to give yourself credit and self-appreciation for this accomplishment. If you can afford it, go out and have a special (and, of course, healthy) lunch, dinner, or smoothie at one of your favorite local establishments, spend time in nature, or indulge in a TV show or movie you have been wanting to see. You deserve this reward (whatever healthy reward you choose), and your mind could use a healthy distraction. Also, by giving yourself a small reward, you will condition your brain to associate pleasure with the develop-mental work you have done and prospectively with the work you will continue to do.

Other than rewarding yourself at the end of Week 1 (or Week 2 if you extended you writings out over two weeks) , the only other assignment you have right after this week is to reread your ideal life (Week 1 – Step 1) before you go to bed. You should read this to yourself, and when you are done reading, you should ask your subconscious mind to work your behalf to move towards the achievement of these goals. This will be a good opportunity for you to start working with your subconscious mind and asking it to work for you. Don't worry – you will likely not receive any type of signal from subconscious that it will do this work for you. All you have to do is politely ask it to help you towards achieving the goals that you desire while you sleep, and it will start working and processing information while you sleep. I am sure you have heard many financial gurus talking about having money working for you while you sleep. Well, now you can you have your most precious investment, you, growing in value while you sleep. I realize this might seem a little too "New-Age" for some of you, but trust me, this will work. Your subconscious mind always wants the best for you. Sometimes, though, your subconscious mind just needs clarity, which you have given it by reading your ideal life Week 1 – Step 1 results, and a little reminding, which you have done by simply asking it to work towards processing this information and moving you in the direction of goal achievement while you sleep.

One item worth noting now is how to deal with some doubts, insecurities, and negative self-talk. For some people, after the initial excitement of the Week 1 exercises starts to settle in, there is an internal doubt and corresponding internal representation that represents doubt and fear. Negative self-talk and unwanted thoughts will naturally occur when you are in a problem state and/or attempting to create change. The Process does not attempt to fight such self-talk or negativity, just acknowledge it. The Process employs a method that consciously avoids such negativity. Over a short time period this method will generalize to the majority your life – effortlessly.

One can express such negative thoughts/feelings in various ways. Still, all such doubts are represented in some form, such as our visual, kinesthetic, or auditory representation – generally a combination of these symbolic systems. For our purposes, we will call these experiences thoughts or unwanted thoughts that express doubt or fear. The intensity, timing and duration of these thoughts will vary by person. These unwanted thoughts are normal and to be expected as you go through such a dramatic change process. As humans, we are hard-wired and conditioned to resist change and hold on to familiarity. It is a human instinct and something that occurs at a subconscious level. Employing the Process will make the change you desire very gentle and organic, and these unwanted thoughts will soon be overwritten by your positive thoughts and experiences.

In the meantime, though, when such thoughts do arise, you are simply to acknowledge these thoughts express some type of internal dialogue such as, "I understand these thoughts are normal, and I am okay with them, as they mean I am in the process of going through a very positive change." You would use this type of self-talk related to any thoughts that relate to the doubt of your abilities to accomplish change or other doubts about the change you want taking place in the future. There will be times during which thoughts of past failures arise. When this happens, simply acknowledge the thought/perceived failure and perform some type of self-talk that basically says, "I understand and accept that happened, and I learned from it." I would sum up this part of the Process in two words – Don't dwell. We don't want to ignore our thoughts or emotional state. We acknowledge them, accept that they are appropriate and expected for where we are in the Process, and they will change and decrease greatly as we continue further in our development. Most importantly, we don't dwell on them – simply acknowledge, accept, and move on! This might seem a bit tedious at first but is important that you be vigilant with gently addressing unwanted doubt/fear thoughts as they arise. This is because, by doing so, you are re-training your mind to react to doubt and fear and training your mind not to be overcome or controlled by doubt and fear. As you start to move closer to your goals and start enjoying the process of change that is taking place as a result of the Process, the frequency of such unwanted thoughts will decrease dramatically.

WEEK 2 - ONGOING STEPS

Moving Toward Your Goals

Life 30 Days From Now

Now that you have completed the initial foundational work of the Process in Week 1, you will start to work on more ongoing journaling that will evolve both over the first

30 days of the Process as well as beyond Day 30, when you are both implementing new behavioral changes as well as maintaining the positive changes you have already implemented.

One of the frameworks of the Process is to chunk up to your higher-level goals and sense of self initially in Week 1. This is done so that you see a clear picture of what is possible and to give your brain a very tangible target to work towards. If you provide your subconscious mind with a specific, tangible outcome, it will work towards this outcome and will find ways for you to achieve it. If we do not come up with a clear specific target, our brain has an infinite amount of choices to move towards, and the likelihood of us achieving what we truly want is very limited and/or random.

While it is essential that you start with big picture targets/goals, it is also necessary for you to chunk these goals down to manageable steps that seem realistic and achievable. That is why the Process looks at your goals from a perspective of six to twelve months out (medium to long-term perspective), and 30 days out (short-term perspective).

Your Week 2 writing/journals involve you writing out what a day in your life will look 30 days from now as you are moving towards the achievement of your goals. It is important to think about this in terms of progress but not completion. There may be some goals that you originally drafted in Week 1 that are completed and close to completed within 30 days, but for the most part, the majority of your goals are in the 'building momentum' stage.

In a journal or the notes pages below, write down a detailed description of a day in your life 30 days from now. This writing is in 1st person and takes the perspective of you having successfully worked towards your goals. It is written from a place of positivity, gratitude, and confidence. This will be redrafted every 30 days. It is important that when you do this initial writing, it again comes from a place of complete positivity. Any potential setback and negative thoughts should be acknowledged mentally but should not be written on paper. The majority of outcomes you are moving towards will very likely be emotional, or feeling-based, meaning that there might be a tangible component associated with them, but we are primarily looking for the feelings or emotional states that these outcomes will gener-ate. These feelings typically are security, companionship, self-respect, higher self-worth, accomplishment, and self-confidence, amongst other feelings/emotional states. Because these feelings are not tangible and are very general, we should focus on specific steps in the process of attaining these feelings/outcomes. It is essential to take the perspec-tive of enjoying the process of achieving your goals when doing this writing, while being specific about steps you are taking so your brain can sense a short-term target to move towards. You should approach this writing from the life perspective of abundance, love, empathy, positivity, and caring.

This can be challenging, but again, this will be consciously performed during short periods and will eventually generalize to a more pervasive state of mind. This journaling requires a very focused state of attention and can feel tedious the first few times you attempt it. With practice, though, this journaling will get easier. One approach to make this journaling easier to imagine as if your very short-term goals or movement towards these goals are met and look backwards from 30 days ahead and see and feel what steps it took to get from where you are now to 30 days ahead. Think of this as backtracking from a future perspective to where you are at now.

A DAY IN YOUR LIFE 30 DAYS FROM NOW WRITING EXERCISE

The Process Notes:

The Process Notes:

The Process Notes:

The Process Notes:

We become what we think about.

Earl Nightingale

MAINTENANCE AND RE-EVALUATION

Week 3 and beyond are maintenance weeks. During this time frame, you should reread your life in 30 days from now before bed and attempt to visualize yourself from an associated perspective (seeing things from the perspective your own eyes as if the event was actually happening). If you have challenges visualizing these items, it is okay – just do your best; your subconscious mind will do the rest. Also, please remember to not only visualize these items but also step in the experience and feel those positive feelings and hear and feel the experience as well. When you are finished visualizing and creating the experience in all senses, turn inwards and ask your subconscious mind to work for you while you are sleeping to process and move towards the attainment of the activities and goals. Your subconscious mind wants to be aligned your true self and desires and will gladly work to help you move towards your goals while you sleep

Each day in the morning, write an abbreviated description of all you will have accomplished during that day that is aligned with positivity, love, inner peace, and moving towards your life 30 days from now. This writing can be very brief, and bullet-pointed. Note the perspective through which this will be written will be after the day is over. This again is reemphasizing training your mind to see the reality of your daily goals and move towards such goals.

At the end of each day, you will also evaluate whether you have made progress on the forecasted actions you wrote down for that day that morning. This should not be done just prior to sleep/bedtime but rather earlier. This is only a feedback mechanism. Do not fret if you did not meet some or all of your goals for the day. As long as you keep doing the other steps in the Process, this will be a reminder to bring more focused states of attention the next day in working towards your goals. This step also allows you to correct your daily writings to make sure you are being realistic in what you can accomplish in a day. Again, I cannot stress enough, this is a feedback tool only. One other note on this topic, I have worked with some people who struggled with this step and still achieved their desired goals. While I would recommend this daily exercise, I realize this is a bit tedious. I recommend trying this exercise and if does not feel right for you to try performing it every couple of days. You are performing this method when you are well into the Process, so you can use your judgement on whether this daily writing exercise feels right for you. If it does not feel right, you can put it aside for now and always revisit it, if you feel you need its' benefits at a later point.

Lastly, at this point, at least once or twice a week before bed, you should read Week 1 Exercise – Your Ideal Life 6 to 12 months from now. You should read this to yourself, and when you are done, you should ask your subconscious mind to work on your behalf to move towards the achievement of these goals.

This may seem like a good deal of daily maintenance, but it really will not take much time. Your reflections before bed should also be very gratifying and enjoyable. They also are likely to result in better and more peaceful sleep. Also, your daily nighttime evaluations will only take a couple minutes, and you should not spend an excessive amount of time on any of these.

POTENTIAL OBSTACLES

There are some typical challenges and obstacles that present themselves during the first week or two of implementing the Process. This is because there is often a time deferral between when you start to make changes and when you internally/mentally start to generalize these changes. They will become more pervasive in your life as time passes. Generally speaking, I am not a big fan of will-power in the context of directly attempting to make behavior changes. In my opinion, there are way too many clinicians that focus exclusively on behavioral change without examining the beliefs and mindset of the person who is attempting to make the behavioral change. With that said, will-power should be utilized for a short period of time in performing the exercises in the Process. Again, this is due to the lag time associated with goal accomplishment and your brain forming a more pervasive positive, authentic goal-oriented mindset. If you find yourself struggling to perform any of the exercises, simply give yourself permission to perform these exercises for a few weeks, knowing that they will absolutely move you towards the right path. The Process has worked for many other people and will work for you as well. Just keep reminding yourself of this if you find yourself starting to lose motivation. Remember that we, as humans, naturally resist change, and if you find yourself skipping a day of exercises or going through them without the full enthusiasm you started with, remember that is not atypical, and you should use will-power for a very short period of time, as this will pay huge dividends for you in the near future. There is virtually no down-side to performing the exercises of the Process consistently. If you are like me and the other people who have utilized the Process, you will see a change in mindset, which will lead to a change in procedures and ulti- mately the results you will achieve. The key is to make your exercises as much a part of your daily routine as brushing your teeth or taking a shower. As long as you are vigilant and persistent through the first several weeks, you will find yourself performing these exercises effortlessly and some- times unconsciously going forward.

During the course of your life, possibly including the timing of your first 30 days implementing the Process, obstacles, setbacks, and other items sometimes outside of your control will occur. Sometimes these obstacles and setbacks will be representative of occurrences that have previously taken place and over which you have no control. Sometimes these obstacles will be external circumstances, such as timing or just bad luck that occur during your attempts to achieve your goals. It is important, no matter what setbacks occur, you accept things the way they are and move forward. There are many NLP teachers who teach that you, as a person, are the cause for everything in your life. While I believe that people will generally find themselves in a much more satisfying position in life if they take accountability and responsibility for the majority of the results in their life. I also believe there are circumstances which are outside of your control and the universe provides us with unpleasant surprises. When this happens, we should accept what the universe has provided us and not to try to use logic to understand why the circumstance happened. When I was diagnosed with cancer, I truly believe this was outside my control. I initially found myself pondering why I would have cancer, how was it possible, and where did it come from? I lived a very healthy lifestyle. I didn't drink, smoke, or do drugs. I had a strict vegan diet. It just didn't make sense for me to get cancer. My pondering, though, did not help me in any way, shape, or form. Soon, though, I realized I would not be able to understand the cause of the cancer, but rather I needed to accept it and view it as a gift to enact other positive changes that I want to make in my life. If during your time implementing the Process, or any other time in your life, you find major obstacles that come your way, I suggest accepting them as being out of your control and utilize the obstacle or situation as motivation to move towards what you truly want or to re-adjust your goals so that they could have a higher purpose as a result of the change in circumstance.

ON-GOING STEPS AFTER THE FIRST 30 DAYS

After completing the first 30 days of the Process, you will have crystal clear clarity of your goals are and, more importantly, why you want to achieve such goals. After you have completed the first 30 days of the Process, you should continue to incorporate the Process into your life. Some of this incorporation will occur at an unconscious level, such as goal setting and positive thinking. At this point, you have a good amount of autonomy in deciding how detailed you want to be with your conscious incorporation of the Process after Day 30. If you find yourself wanting to continue the daily journaling exercises, feel free to do them; this can only be beneficial. If you find yourself wanting to do occasional exercises, that will work as well. What is most important, beyond Day 30, is that you utilize self-awareness and flexibility. For example, if you find that you are falling off track with your goals, you might want to revisit the daily exercises (both written and non-written). Also, if you find that your goals need adjustment because of situational changes in your life (both good and bad), you might want to restart the process from the beginning so that you have a more updated representation of your goals. At a minimum, though, I would suggest once per month you write out a day in your ideal life 30 days from that point and continue to reflect on this prior to bedtime, asking your subconscious mind to move you in the direction of this ideal life and related goals. You should

also try to reflect on your ideal life 6 to 12 months out
(Week 1- Day 1) every night before bed and continue to ask
your subconscious mind to propel you towards this desired
life. Also, assuming everything else is on target, you should
consider redrafting your ideal life 6 to 12 months out (Week
1- Day 1) at least twice per year.

The Process Notes:

The Process Notes:

The Process Notes:

The Process Notes:

Chapter 11

CONCLUSION

"Take Pictures-Not of Sights. Don't Take Pictures of Buildings. Take Pictures of Moments, Because That's What Matters."

James Roday portraying fictional character
Shawn Spencer on television show Psych.

You now have completed 30 days' worth of work utilizing the Process. You utilized a very tangible framework that was very gentle, yet at the same time, was built off of the momentum of reprogramming your perspective over a 30-day period. This work you did was very deep and much beyond just surface-level endeavors. It started with clearly defining what you wanted (desired state/out-come), aligning this with your sense of self or your true identity. From there, you chunked your long-term goals into short-term steps in a manner that fully enjoyed the process of working towards your goals. You have done all this with a positive attitude and mindset, and while there were distractions, doubts, fears, and even negative self-talk along the way, following the framework of the Process allowed you to not be consumed by such limitations and also allowed for the positivity present during the Process to generalize and become more pervasive in all aspects of your life. You no doubt feel more empowered, accomplished, driven, and motivated after just 30 days of following the steps of the Process. The hard work is over now, and you simply need to take simple steps to maintain the positive and goal-oriented attitude that you have imprinted upon yourself in the last 30 days. In the previous chapter of this book, you will find simple instructions on how to maintain and build upon the powerful work you completed so far. When doing so, it is essential you celebrate your successes, remain open to new possibilities that life will bring, recognize the progress you have made, and above all, be flexible and adaptable, as life inevitably changes and brings you new challenges and new opportunities.

Remember, the Process is exactly what it is titled - "a process." It is not a destination, although you will reach many desired destinations and outcomes using the Process.

The short-term goal of the Process was to help you achieve the goals you wanted over the short and medium term, but perhaps the biggest impact the Process will have on you is the shift in your thought processes about what is possible, how easy it is to achieve by following simple steps, and the creation of a life-long mindset of positivity, abundance, gratitude, and empowerment, which will, in turn, allow you to continually and easily achieve your desired outcomes as your life progresses.

While some of the detailed steps described in the Process may seem arduous or overwhelming at times, please try your best to follow them but know, different approaches work for different people. If you are in doubt about what you should read one day or reflect before bed etc., just choose something positive that you have written. I always default back to a day in your ideal life 6 to 12 months from now. If in doubt, reread that before bed or when you are feeling the need during the day. When you get to the point of writing your ideal day in your life 30 days from now, reread that too. If you are stuck on what you should be writing, simply write something completely positive about what your life is already starting to look like in the future. You can always revisit the text of the book at a later time and follow the sequential steps then. What I am saying here is basically yes, I highly recommend sticking to the sequence of the steps presented but if you get confused on this, don't get frustrated, just follow the basic principles and something positive will come from this. If you are stuck on what to write, just journal something positive. The further along you get in the Process, the less the actual exercise specifics matter versus understanding the structure behind the exercise. This understanding will happen organically over time.

As new goals and challenges arise in your life, I encourage you to revisit the Process and reimplement it contextually to your new goals. Review your previous writings/journals and use these as a starting point when implementing new goals/positive changes. You will be amazed at how much you can leverage off of what you have previously written/explored and just make little tweaks in your writings to make them contextually specific to your new goal.

Lastly, I would like to state that the Process is more than just what you read in this book and the journaling and exercises you went through. Those are extremely important and by all means necessary. In addition, though, I am very sure early on into your journey with this book, you figured out the methods and frameworks discussed are really a way of life. A simple way of life. Yes, I explain the rationale for the methods, and this helps to motivate you. Even though I criticized mere motivational books, motivation is important, so I added direct and embedded motivational language to this book to help you along the journey. Again, all that helps, but what this book really comes down to is you helping yourself, even in the roughest of times, by doing a couple simple yet challenging things. Always maintain a positive mindset. As soon you notice that positive mindset slipping, reset and move on – don't dwell. Don't dwell on the past – learn from it to set tangible goals. Bring your positive mindset to those goals. Don't be selfish. Make sure your goals support others. Check in on your goals periodically to make sure they still support the current you and your tribe. Find your path. Be flexible enough to recalibrate and change your path. Help others. Be kind. Love others freely. Love your life! I promise you if you do all these things, most of the time (no one is perfect), you will find yourself living an unbelievable life (on your own terms), surrounded by great people, situations, and opportunities. You will be able to handle challenges with much more ease. You will be more confident in the face of adversity. You will have an inner peace and stability that people can sense. You deserve all this and more. Many blessings on your path!

The Process Notes:

The Process Notes:

The Process Notes:

The Process Notes:

OTHER PERSONAL THOUGHTS TO HELP ON YOUR
JOURNEY/PATH

"There are a lot of paths out there – You just got to choose your own."

Johnny Utah – Fictional Character – Point
Break 2015 -Deleted Scenes

These are all just suggestions of items that I personally find rewarding for myself. I wanted to share this to spark some ideas and so you could get a glimpse of what makes me tick. Again, follow your own path.

- **Meditate.** I try to meditate at least once daily for 15 minutes. There are tons of YouTube videos on meditation. Brendon Burchard does a really good video on meditation that I like. His work seems to resemble transcendental meditation. I would also recommend looking into this. I would also recommend listening to the works of Gabrielle Bernstein, who is also a good source for both meditation and spiritual awakening materials.
- **Learn Non-violent Communication** – This is an effective way to communicate with others, especially those who you are in close relationships with.
- **Learn NLP.** I am biased here, and you can clearly see my affiliation to NLP. I highly recommend anything put out by NLP Comprehensive.
- **Be conscious about what you eat.** If you really think about the practice of eating animals and the pain and suffering it causes, you would find a shift towards a more humane, healthy, and conscious diet.
- **Do what makes you happy** – If something doesn't make you happy, avoid it. This does not mean you can avoid necessary chores or work, etc. What it does mean, though, is you only have

limited time on this Earth. Choose wisely how you want to spend your time.

- **Don't get too caught up with money** – Most self-help practitioners don't share this philosophy. They will tell you your balance sheet is proportionate to the value you add, and in order to serve, you have to have a direct relationship with high income/financial asset accumulation. My personal view, based on my own learning experiences, is that too much of an emphasis on money will drive you to make monetary mistakes. Look – you need money to live; just don't end up worshipping it. Do what you love and don't put money as your first criterion for how you run your life.

- **Love openly. Don't judge. Be kind**– show empathy.

- **Read often** – I will be putting a book list on my website, social media, or somewhere that is very easily found.

- **Learn about spirituality** – Be careful here. Your beliefs are your beliefs. If you are already comfortable with your spirituality/religious beliefs, that is great. If not, I would encourage you to explore the various spiritual and religious platforms out there. Just be careful. As I said, every spiritual path is not for everyone, and sadly, this area is not very regulated, so be sure to practice due diligence when exploring spiritual beliefs and pathways - choose very carefully.

- **Spend time in nature** – Appreciate Mother Earth and all of her gifts (all of the plants and animals on this planet). Find the beauty in them. Think about this beauty the next time you want to eat an animal product.
- **Do a daily gratitude list**
- **Daily exercise** – I personally love martial arts and basketball.
- **Declutter your space** – don't get caught up with consumerism. Before you purchase something, ask yourself if you really need it. A decluttered area will help clear your mind for fresh thoughts. I am inherently disorganized, so I get how hard this is, but it will be worth it.
- **Don't compare yourself to others**. Everyone is on their own path. Following the framework of this book will help you realize yours.
- **Help others wherever you can** – Trust in indirect karma.
- **Put yourself in positive environments.** Environment is a key factor in your development.
- **Take the time to get to know someone** you

might have always not liked or not got along with. Try to take their perspective.

- **Support your local economy.**
- **Learn a new skill that you enjoy** – Approach it with child-like openness.

BIBLIOGRAPHY

Chapter 1 and 3 -

Tony Robbins: The 6 Basic Needs that Make us Tick – Entrepreneur Magazine- 2014; https://www.tonyrobbins. com/mind-meaning/do-you-need-to-feel-significant/

Chapter 6 –

The Power of Full Engagement: Managing Energy, Not Time, is the Key to High Performance and Personal Renewal Loehr and Schwartz (2003) Free Press Publishing

Charlie Minanno is a vegan and a cancer survivor. He is an entrepreneur and currently consults as an Organizational Psychologist. Charlie has consulted with various companies ranging from local holistic businesses to PwC and many businesses in between. He has been a life-long student of Neuro linguistic programming (NLP) and has facilitated many NLP study groups and workshops. His interests are varied and range from the mundane, such as basketball and economics, to more esoteric studies. An animal rights proponent and animal lover, Charlie lives just outside of Philadelphia, PA.